Facts About the Downy Woodpecker

By Lisa Strattin

© 2016 Lisa Strattin

Revised © 2020

FREE BOOK

FOR ALL SUBSCRIBERS

LisaStrattin.com/Subscribe-Here

FACTS ABOUT THE
SKUNK

A PICTURE BOOK FOR KIDS

Lisa Strattin

Facts for Kids Picture Books by Lisa Strattin

Pygmy Rabbit, Vol 153

Jumping Rabbit, Vol 154

Mini Rabbits, Vol 155

Blue Quail, Vol 156

Mountain Quail, Vol 157

Quokka, Vol 158

Quoll, Vol 159

Raccoon, Vol 160

Raccoon Dog, Vol 161

Radiated Tortoise, Vol 162

Sign Up for New Release Emails Here

http://LisaStrattin.com/subscribe-here

All information in this book has been carefully researched and checked for factual accuracy. However, the author and publisher makes no warranty, express or implied, that the information contained herein is appropriate for every individual, situation or purpose and assume no responsibility for errors or omissions. The reader assumes the risk and full responsibility for all actions, and the author will not be held responsible for any loss or damage, whether consequential, incidental, special or otherwise, that may result from the information presented in this book.

All images are free for use or purchased from stock photo sites or royalty free for commercial use.

Some coloring pages might be of the general species due to lack of available images.

I have relied on my own observations as well as many different sources for this book and I have done my best to check facts and give credit where it is due. In the event that any material is used without proper permission, please contact me so that the oversight can be corrected.

Contents

INTRODUCTION

The Downy Woodpecker is the smallest of Washington's woodpeckers. Its plumage is a mix of black and white. The wings, lower back, and tail are black with white spots; the upper back and outer tail feathers are white. Its underside is white, and its head is marked with wide alternating black and white stripes.

Males have a red spot on the back of their head which females don't have. Downy Woodpeckers resemble the larger Hairy Woodpeckers, but Downys have relatively smaller bills, which give their heads a rounder, 'cuter' shape.

Downy Woodpeckers found in western Washington are considerably darker than the ones found in eastern Washingto, with most of the areas described above as 'white' actually being a dingy tan. Juveniles look like adults but may have red on their foreheads.

INTERESTING FACTS

In the winters, Downy Woodpeckers are frequent members of mixed species flocks. Male and female Downy Woodpeckers divide up the areas where they search for food during the winter. Males feed more on small branches and weed stems, and females feed on larger branches and trunks. Males will block the females from foraging in the better spots. The Downy Woodpecker eats foods that larger woodpeckers cannot reach, like the insects living on or in the stems of weeds.

Woodpeckers don't sing songs, but they drum loudly against pieces of wood or metal to achieve the same effect. Downy Woodpeckers have been discovered nesting inside the walls of buildings.

SHAPE AND SIZE

Downy Woodpeckers are small versions of the classic woodpecker. They have a straight, chisel-like bill, blocky head, wide shoulders, and straight-backed posture as they lean away from tree limbs and onto their tail feathers.

The bill tends to look smaller for the bird's size than in other woodpeckers. Adult downy woodpeckers are the smallest of North America's woodpeckers. The total length of the species ranges from 5.5 to 7.1 inches and the wingspan from 9.8 to 12 inches. Their body weight ranges from just over 1/2 ounce to 1 ounce.

DIET

Downy Woodpeckers eat insects, especially beetles and ants. They also feed on berries, seeds, and suet.

LIFE CYCLE

It takes less than 1 year for a Downy Woodpecker to be ready to have babies. Spring and early summer is the time when they usually lay their eggs. Each egg takes 12 days to hatch and they stay with their parents for about a month.

LIFE SPAN

The lifespan of a Downy Woodpecker ranges from 4-11 years in the wild. The oldest known Downy Woodpecker was a male and at least 11 years, 11 months old when he was re-captured and re-released during banding operations in California.

SOCIAL BEHAVIOR

Downy woodpeckers are active during the daytime. They stay in the same general area all year and do not migrate to other climates. They are solitary and territorial. Males will defend their territory against other males, and females defend a territory against other females. When an intruder enters a downy woodpecker's territory, the resident woodpecker uses threat displays, such as wing flicking, or fanning their tail, raising their crest and holding their bill high to try to drive the intruder away. If threat displays do not work, downy woodpeckers may attack the intruder, grappling with them in mid-air.

Downy woodpeckers use calls and body signals to communicate. They produce a variety of sounds, including "pik", rattle, scolding, "wad", "chirp", squeak, screech, and distress calls. The "pik" call introduces the rattle call, and these are used during aggressive interactions. Short calls, the "wad" and "chirp", are uttered by young birds. A longer note call, the squeak, is also uttered by young downy woodpeckers. The screech and distress calls are used to signal alarm.

Drumming is a common non-vocal sound that downy woodpeckers use to communicate with each other. This sound is used most often in late winter and spring. This sound is what they use to establish and defend a territory, to attract a mate, and to communicate between mates.

Downy woodpeckers also use body postures to communicate. Bill pointing and waving, wing flicking, crest raising, wing spreading, tail spreading, head turning and head swinging are some of the body postures that downy woodpeckers use to communicate, whether aggressively or as friendly gestures.

SUITABILITY AS PETS

Downy Woodpeckers prefer deciduous trees rather than conifers, so if you live near conifer trees, it may take some time for them to find your feeder. Downy Woodpeckers adore suet and they're common visitors at suet feeders. They also like seeds (corn and black oil sunflower). Putting out some suet and birdseed will get satisfying results if you want to watch these birds.

COLOR ME

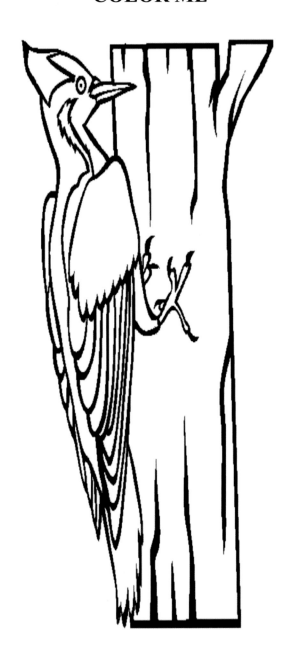

COLOR ME

COLOR ME

COLOR ME

COLOR ME

Please leave me a review here:

http://lisastrattin.com/Review-Vol-37

For more Kindle Downloads Visit Lisa Strattin Author Page on Amazon Author Central

http://amazon.com/author/lisastrattin

To see upcoming titles, visit my website at LisaStrattin.com– all books available on kindle!

http://lisastrattin.com

FREE BOOK

FOR ALL SUBSCRIBERS

LisaStrattin.com/Subscribe-Here

Made in the USA
Monee, IL
24 January 2022

89796856R00024